Teenage Refugees From

BOSNIA-HERZEGOVINA

Speak Out

IN THEIR OWN VOICES

Teenage Refugees From
BOSNIA-
HERZEGOVINA
Speak Out

Valerie Tekavec

GLOBE FEARON EDUCATIONAL PUBLISHER
A Division of Simon & Schuster
Upper Saddle River, New Jersey

Published in 1995 by The Rosen Publishing Group, Inc.
29 East 21st Street, New York, New York 10010

First Edition

Manufactured in the United States of America.

Library of Congress Cataloging-in-Publication Data

Teenage refugees from Bosnia-Herzegovina speak out / Valerie Tekavec. — 1st ed.
    p.   cm. — (In their own voices)
Includes bibliographical references and index.
ISBN 0-835-91121-7
1. Bosnian American teenagers—Juvenile literature. 2. Refugees—United States—Juvenile literature. [Bosnian Americans. 2. Refugees. 3. Youths' writings.] I. Tekavec, Valerie. II. Series.
E184.B67T45 1995
305.23'5'0899182073—dc20   94-40369
                                                                     CIP
                                                                     AC

Contents

Smoke rises over the city of Sarajevo in early 1994 after heavy shelling forced residents to remain indoors.

INTRODUCTION

Bosnia-Herzegovina is an ethnic and religious riddle. At least, that is how it appears to many people. A civil war is raging there. The riddle centers on the rivalry between different nationalities living in one country, and the results of a long and complicated political and religious history. If the riddle could be solved, many people would be relieved of their misery.

The best way to describe the country is "diverse." Before the war, Bosnia-Herzegovina was home to about 4,500,000 people: Serbs, Croats, Muslims, Jews, Albanians, Bulgarians, Hungarians, Macedonians, Montenegrins, Slovaks, and Slovenes.

Many of the kids you will meet in this book are victims of the problems that occur when society is not capable of ethnic and religious tolerance. These teenagers ended up as refugees, a deeply traumatic experience. Tremendous losses are involved: loss of home, loved ones, livelihood, culture.

Bosnia-Herzegovina was a republic of Yugoslavia before national and religious conflicts began to emerge. As early as 1989, and perhaps even earlier, tensions were mounting between the national groups in Yugoslavia. War broke out in 1990, and eventually the republics of Slovenia, Croatia, Serbia, and Montenegro seceded, declaring themselves independent states.

Bosnia-Herzegovina also became an independent country, and it has become the central battleground of the ongoing war. The fighting involves the country's three major national groups: the Serbs, the Croats, and the Muslims. The Muslims make up 40 percent of the country's population; the Serbs account for another third, while the Croats amount to about one fifth.

The basic battle involves territory. The war tactics have been hideous. Brutal campaigns by the different armies have been reported. Prisoners in prison camps have been executed, tortured, raped, and starved. Muslims, Croats, and Serbs have experienced and committed atrocities. This book is intended to give each group a chance to speak.

An ethnic map of Bosnia-Herzegovina resembles a quilt, with large Serb communities living in the northwest and smaller pockets in the east and southern tip of the country. The Muslims live primarily in the far northwest and in specific areas all over eastern and central Bosnia-Herzegovina. The Croats occupy a large area on the eastern side of the Dinaric Alps, on the border of Croatia, as well as areas in the southwest and central regions. The major cities of Bosnia-Herzegovina are home to all three groups.

Croatian President Franjo Tudjman, left, shakes the hand of Bosnian President Alija Izetbegovic in 1994. They met to discuss a Muslim-Croat federation.

*Zrno po zrno — pogača,
kamen po kamen — palača*

ENGLISH TRANSLATION FROM SERBO-CROAT:
Grain by grain—a loaf of bread,
stone by stone—a house is made.

The problems besetting Bosnia-Herzegovina are in no way recent. The country lies precisely in the region that divides the Christian world from Islam. It also marks the separation between Rome and Constantinople—or the Catholic and Eastern Orthodox religions—which occurred in the Great Schism in 1472. Various external powers have wrestled over the Balkan region for centuries. The patchwork settlement of the land reflects this.

The Muslim population in Bosnia-Herzegovina are descendants of the indigenous Slavs who converted to Islam at the time of the Ottoman invasions in the 16th century. Thus they share an ethnic background with the Serbs and Croats. This shared heritage adds an ironic twist to the struggle between the nationalities.

The important thing now is to listen to the Bosnians. Whether someone is Croat, Muslim, or Serb, he or she has most certainly experienced pain and misunderstanding. The kids in this book have a lot to tell about their experiences as refugees. They have left a country in shambles and don't know if they will ever return. Perhaps there is no immediate solution to the riddle of Bosnia-Herzegovina, but listening to its voices might be a good beginning.

Some of the teenagers interviewed for this book asked that their photographs not be used. Others wanted the world to know who they are. In all cases, we have used only the students' first names in order to protect their privacy.

Many of the teenagers in this book are Bosnian Muslims. This is a reflection of the current pattern of immigration from Bosnia to the U.S.◆

Enisa is a young poet. Her poems have been published in Serbo-Croat and in French translation.

Enisa is very close to her family. Her story shows how, in the face of complete loss, family is what matters most.

When Enisa arrived in New York City in August 1993, 200,000 people had already died in the war in Bosnia. She talks about the death of her generation and how it will affect the country and her city, Sarajevo.

To My Generation by Enisa Begic

Silence and peace in schools,
Dust and shame in a street,
Who is going to the prom
With dead graduates?

Their dreams, words and happiness
Have ended too early,
The ones from the mountain
Struck youth of Sarajevo,
Wounded it and took its joy.

I am slowly wandering around Sarajevo
Looking at the dusty, flat field;
A school was once here,
Neither school nor half of students
Are here now.

I feel tears rolling down my face,
I am trying to see the cowards
Who killed youth of 'my' city,
Where so many children were lost
Without any trace.

ENISA
LIFE IN SARAJEVO

I had a wonderful life in Sarajevo before the war broke out. My school and teachers were great. We lived in a wonderful part of town. We had a big four-bedroom apartment on two floors. There was a lot of green around. I had everything that I wished for. My parents had great jobs. My mother is a nurse. My father is a mechanical engineer.

In the winter, my sister and I used to go skiing in the mountains outside the city. It was a real American dream, my life in Sarajevo. You know, you always hear that America is the dream, America is great. But I had my America there. I was so happy.

Religion and nationality were unimportant to my parents and me. What was important was that people were good. I never even knew if some of my friends were Serbs or Croats. I didn't even want to know. I still love them, and I know they are not

13

guilty of what has happened. My best friend is Croat, but she tells me she doesn't feel like a Croat. She's Catholic and from Bosnia.

I lived in Ilidza, a part of Sarajevo where a lot of Serbs lived. I am Muslim. Everything was peaceful between us, but when the war started, Serbs changed. They didn't want to talk to me any more. They didn't want to come to my house any more. Then many Serbs started sending their children away to Serbia. I couldn't believe it. School was going to start in a few days, and all the children were gone. I looked around my empty neighborhood and asked myself "Why? Why?"

The day I left Sarajevo it was raining. I was crying. I felt I was looking at it for the last time. We had to leave at the last moment. I went with my father and my sister to Trogir, a town in Croatia near Split. My mother stayed on because she's a nurse. We thought we would come back to Bosnia, but it didn't turn out that way.

My mother was working in a mobile unit in Ilidza. There were Serb nationalists everywhere. Ten days later, the doctor told my mother and the staff they shouldn't come to the unit any more because they might be taken hostage.

My mother heard shooting everywhere. Our very good neighbor, the principal of my elementary school, a Muslim, was killed by the gym teacher of the same school. My mother came to Croatia on the last train to leave Sarajevo. After that, the station was burned.

Muslim and Croatian prisoners at a detention camp near Sarajevo carry food for their meals.

In those ten days before she came to Croatia, I found out what "mother" means. My sister and I couldn't eat. We just cried the whole time. We blamed my father that she stayed. When she did make it to Trogir, I was very happy.

I have been in the United States for one month. Last week we found out that my grandfather died. He had cancer. Before we left, he said he knew he was going to die and he wanted to die in his country. Now he's gone. I always dreamed that I would see him again. It is very painful.

I was in the best high school in Sarajevo. I wanted to study medicine. It was as if my dream broke. I feel as if I've lost everything.

15

Two Bosnian students prepare for school to open again. Their school was renamed for a teacher who was killed in a Serbian attack.

I finished my last year of high school in Croatia. It was relatively peaceful there between people. But when my mother went to enroll me, the school principal asked, "What are you?" She answered, "I am a Bosnian refugee." He said, "I know that, but *what* are you; what is your religion?" When she told him we were Muslim, he said I couldn't go to that school. "We have no place for Muslims."

My mother is a very strong woman. She didn't want to tell me about the school; she just said I might have difficulty getting in.

But then we met a great man, a math teacher at the school. When he saw my school records from Bosnia, he said he would do everything he could to get me into the school. He couldn't believe the principal had said no.

I was so broken in Croatia. It was as if I had lost my heart. I felt like an old woman. I didn't go anywhere. I only had a few friends I saw at school. I watched the news all day, and I cried. I cried all the time, all day long. I kept dreaming of my house, my Sarajevo. I talked only about my Sarajevo.

So many young people in Sarajevo have died. Someone wrote to us that the generation of boys between 1968 and 1976 is dead. Sometimes I ask myself, "How did this happen? How did my friends, Muslims and Serbs, take sides and start killing each other?"

We had a series of interviews with the United Nations office in Croatia before we came to New York. The immigration office found an apartment for us, and they gave us $480 for food; that was supposed to last us two months. There was no furniture. They told us to sleep on the floor.

We were lucky to meet some people from Bosnia who had lived here for years. All we had were our bags. We had no money, nothing. It was like starting over again. They helped us find a better apartment and even helped us get furniture. We are so happy now. We have everything we need.

I have a job at McDonald's, here in the Bronx. They call me when they need me, not every day, sometimes three hours, sometimes seven hours. I make French fries. I work at the register. Whatever they want I do. It's good.

My father just got a job today. He is washing glasses in a restaurant. He never washed a single glass at home! He's probably broken one by now!

I love New York City very much. In the weeks before we left Croatia, I heard people saying bad things about Muslims all the time. It was very upsetting. On the airplane, the flight attendants were so nice to me. As we were getting off the plane, they started to cry. When that happened I thought, "I will love America, and America is going to love me." It was an important moment for me. I'll never forget it.

I am very happy that I'm here. I've had so much good luck that I'm almost afraid. I feel different here. I am stronger. When I think of America, I think, "America is the sister of my Bosnia." We will be in America until Bosnia is ready to take us back.

Sometimes I lose hope that I will ever go back. But then I think, how stupid and terrible of me. All those people are fighting in Sarajevo, and here I am losing hope. I know it won't be the same when I go back. It will be better, or it will be worse. I do not know.

All my friends write to me. They are refugees, too. They write from all over the world, Switzerland, Venezuela. They all say, "We will go back someday to our Sarajevo." I know we will go back and we will rebuild our Sarajevo and our Bosnia.◆

Josip Broz Tito served as prime minister of Yugoslavia for 35 years, after establishing a Communist government there near the end of World War II.

Ljubica is a Serbian refugee living in Virginia. Ljubica is a bright, energetic girl who has managed to support herself and go to school entirely alone in the United States. The rest of her family is still in Bosnia.

She talks a lot about the American media and their coverage of the war in Bosnia. Her views are penetrating and insightful. She believes that the Serbs as a group are portrayed negatively.

Ljubica also struggles with national prejudice. Coming from a place filled with rage, she tries not to fall into long-established patterns of hatred between the national groups. She is very honest about how it affects her internally, but she also believes it is necessary to retain one's identity.

LJUBICA

WHAT AM I?

My name is Ljubica. I had just turned 18 when I came to the United States. I am from a small town not far from Banja Luka. I came to the U.S. as an exchange student, and I lived with a family in a little town outside Philadelphia.

I went to high school there for a year. The first four months were nice. I was meeting people, making friends. I was a normal teenager, I guess. But I wasn't happy with many things in America. It's not easy to make good friends here. I mostly made friends with other exchange students.

Then the war broke out. I remember talking to my dad on the phone in the spring. I asked him if anything was going on in my town, and he said, "No, everything's fine!" But it was close. There was fighting right across the river, on the border between Bosnia and Croatia.

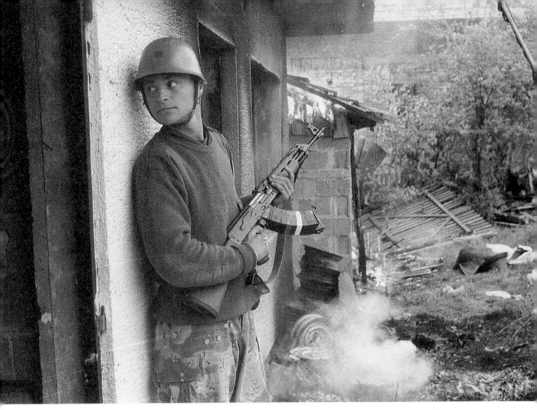

A Serbian soldier takes cover behind a burning house in a Bosnian village.

About a month after we spoke, the phone lines were disconnected, and I knew that they were in the war. I was unable to contact my family from April to September in 1992.

My exchange year in the U.S. was coming to a close, and when it was time for me to leave, I didn't know where to go. So I applied for political asylum in the U.S. I got my employment authorization. A month later, I got a job as a nanny. I worked for a couple in Philadelphia with two little kids. Then I moved with them to Washington, D.C. All this time I didn't know anything about my parents. It was the worst five months of my life.

I remember my 19th birthday, in July. I was

writing a letter to my parents. I wrote to my old

address, although I didn't know if it would get through. It was a very emotional letter. I cried all over it. The paper was wet.

My parents got the letter at the end of August, two days before my father had to go to the front lines to fight. They read it and cried. Dad said he would go to the front and fight once more, and when he came back he would get right into the car and go get me. But he was wounded. It was a miracle that he survived.

My father is committed to staying in Bosnia. I hope to go back, too. But now I'm going to a community college in Falls Church, Virginia. I'm doing general studies. I plan to stay in the U.S. until I finish a four-year degree somewhere.

My people have a lot to offer me. We have a very rich culture. We're very intelligent people. And we're very good-hearted, even though we're getting this bad rap right now. We have children, we love our children. We go to church, we listen to music. We are people, but we're being portrayed as animals.

Now, when people say Bosnia is this multi-cultural country where everybody got along, it's a huge lie. You always knew who was a Muslim, who was a Serb, who was a Croat. And you got along nicely as long as you didn't marry them. It's the same as the Jewish-Catholic thing here. I'm not saying it's right, but that's the way it is. What's happening in Bosnia is going on in other places in the world. It got violent in my country, but the violence could happen anywhere else, too.

It's been very hard for me and my Bosnian friends living here in the United States. When you say, "I'm from Yugoslavia," the question, "From what part of Yugoslavia?" always follows. When you answer, "Bosnia," the person says, "Oh! What are you?" When I answer, "Serbian," people say things like, "Oh! You're the bad guys!"

This has happened to me hundreds of times. People condemn the whole nation for something they don't even know about. Like the 60,000 rapes: A report by the United Nations states that a total of 800 rapes occurred in Bosnia, 350 of which they have evidence for. It also states that all sides had an equal part in it.

People in Bosnia are dying, and it's very bad. But people overlook that people in Serbia are dying, too. Children are dying because of the sanctions. People don't have food, basic medical supplies. I don't understand the purpose for cutting them off. Sometimes, I think, "I'm so sick of the words 'Muslim,' 'Serbian,' 'Croatian,' 'NATO.'" That's my life, the war. It's not very pleasant. The bookshelves in my room are lined with books like *The State of Croatia* or *The Serbs.*

I still hang out with a lot of Yugoslavians. We get into discussions sometimes and we argue. If

A refugee holds her two-month-old baby as another woman prepares baby food. They are among many refugees who have fled the Bihac area of Bosnia.

somebody says the Serbs are the ones who are doing all the killing, I get very mad. But if someone says everyone is a victim, you have your goal, we have ours, I react pretty calmly. I can see that I'm talking to a rational person. I'm not a crazy nationalist. I believe that it's fine to be proud of who you are, as long as you don't intrude on anyone else's national feelings.

I think American kids should try to overcome their ignorance. They should read about Bosnian history, like Ivo Andric's book *The Bridge on the Drina.* People should learn something about Bosnia and the Serbs before they hang them.◆

Alexander is thirteen years old. He is a Croat and comes from a town that had a mainly Croat population. When he first left his country, he was a refugee in Croatia. Many Bosnian-Croats have moved to neighboring Croatia as refugees. Unlike the Muslims, the Croats and Serbs have had "sister countries" to flee to. But it didn't work out in Croatia for Alexander's family and they had to move on. So they came to Canada.

ALEXANDER
LEAVING BIHAC

My name is Alexander. I come from Bihac, a town in northwestern Bosnia-Herzegovina. Bihac is very close to the Croatian border, on the Una River. I live in Toronto, Canada, now. My mother's sister sponsored me and my family to come here. My aunt has been in Canada for six years.

Becoming a refugee was a big change in my life. I came to a new city. I didn't speak English very well, and I didn't have any friends. I've been here for eight months now and have some friends. That makes things a little easier. My new friends are Canadian, Polish, and Chinese.

There was a lot of fighting in Bihac in the war, but I left before it started. There were Serbs, Croats, and Muslims living in my town, but the largest group was Croatian. I am Croatian, too.

The Croatian city of Dubrovnik was shelled by the Yugoslav federal army in 1991.

I left Bihac almost three years ago. At first I lived in Croatia, in Zagreb, with my mother and my sister. We stayed there for two years. It was a very difficult time. My father couldn't come with us. The Serbs in Bosnia wouldn't let him cross the border into Croatia. I still haven't seen my father since we left Bihac, and for a long time it was impossible to reach him by phone or letter.

The last year we spent in Zagreb we had refugee status. We were very hungry. There was no food, no coal, no wood, nothing. Now we are doing much better, and my father will be arriving in Toronto in a few days. I am very excited, because my family will finally be back together again. He was wounded in the war, but he is O.K.

Right now I'm taking ESL at my school. My English is getting better. My favorite subject is math. When I was in Bosnia I liked history, and I used to play soccer and basketball. In Toronto, I like to play ice hockey, but they don't offer soccer at my school. After school I like to watch TV.

When we lived in Bosnia, my mother was a social worker. My father drove a truck. Right now my mother is working at the Croatian Club in Toronto. When I am older, I would like to be a cop.

There are very few Croats living in Bihac now. Many have left the town as refugees and have gone to live in Croatia. I don't think I will ever go back to Bosnia. I will stay in Canada. There is nothing left for me in Bosnia.◆

Jasmin has been in the United States for only a short time. He is Muslim. The journey from his village in western Bosnia to his new home in Utica, New York, took seven months. When Jasmin arrived with his family, they had no home, no jobs, and no knowledge of English. The resettlement agency in Utica helped them find a home in Corn Hill, an old, economically depressed area where 65 percent of the houses are abandoned. The neighborhood is known for its refugee community.

Jasmin is an intense young man. He and his family experienced much physical and emotional strain in Bosnia. Yet, despite the hardship, he maintains an awesome stoicism. His rigid manner and clipped language hint at fresh wounds yet to heal.

JASMIN
NIGHTS IN THE FOREST

I am Jasmin. I come from Ramic, a village in western Bosnia, near the city of Kljuch. My village is a good size. There are 100 houses and three or four roads. Ramic is a very beautiful place. It lies on the slope of a small hill. The country is very green.

I am now here in Utica, New York, with my family. I have a brother and a sister. My grandmother and my uncle live with us, too. I am the oldest child. I am 18.

I arrived as a refugee in the United States a little more than a month ago. When I left Bosnia, I left many friends behind. They are scattered, as refugees, all over the world, in France, in Canada, in Germany. Some of them are still in Bosnia, fighting in the war.

I went to elementary school in my village. I was a good student there. I received the highest grades. When I turned 13, I went to another school in a nearby village, Velegici. Later, until the war broke out, I went to school in Kljuch, seven kilometers

Sarajevo residents run to avoid sniper fire in the city's infamous "Sniper Alley."

away. I took the bus there every day. My favorite subjects are math, physics, and chemistry. I also like sports, especially soccer.

When the war started, my school was suddenly closed and barricaded. All over Bosnia, people started taking sides. Provocations began in my village, and the Yugoslavian army came in. Certain Muslims in the village killed three soldiers. That is when the trouble really began. After that incident, I, my father, my uncle, and others were arrested. One of the people who arrested us was our next-door neighbor. I was released the following day, but they locked up my father and uncle in a cell in Novo Gradiska. Some days later they were taken to a camp in the city of Banja Luka, where 4,500 people were imprisoned. They held my father and uncle for seven months.

Meanwhile, I was in my village with the rest of my family. At night, many houses were burned down and destroyed. I was afraid, so I spent the nights in the woods with about 15 other boys. My sister, mother, and brother stayed at home.

The people of Kljuch are mostly Serbian. Many of the surrounding villages are Muslim. I am Muslim. In some of the villages, particularly in Velegici, hundreds of people were killed. The night I was arrested, I saw dead people in the streets.

After some weeks, we were granted passage to Croatia. We had to pay 50 German marks each to cross the border. That was a lot of money for us. We wrote to the Red Cross that our home in Ramic had been burned down. They gave us food packages in Zagreb and helped in reuniting us with my father and uncle. We lived in Zagreb for three months before my father and uncle were released from the prison camp. During that time, I worked at a construction site, ten hours a day.

When my father and uncle joined us in Zagreb, they were in bad shape. They had suffered dearly in Banja Luka. They had been given one slice of bread a day to share among four people. Many prisoners died of illness and beatings. My father and uncle were both badly beaten. When he came to Zagreb, my father had three broken ribs and open wounds on his nose and head. We spent the rest of our days in Zagreb normally, with no fighting or war.

We left Croatia by bus, traveling first to Vienna. From there we took a plane to Amsterdam, on to New York, and then to Syracuse.

Right now, I spend my days studying English. It's not difficult to learn, because I have studied a foreign language before. I had Russian for six years in school.

I haven't been in Utica long enough to have many impressions. Everything is so new. I have made some friends at my school where I study English. Most of them are refugees from other countries.

Nationally, I consider myself a Bosnian, even though the concept "Bosnian" doesn't exist any more for many people of my country. Before the war, I lived and spoke with people of different religions and nationalities. We were all living together, Muslims, Croats, and Serbs.

What I want most for myself is to learn English, graduate from high school, and get a job. What I want most for Bosnia is to be free and united. I don't want the country to be divided. Someday I want to go back. I miss Bosnia. I miss the people and how they were before the war.◆

The 1984 Winter Olympic Games were held in Sarajevo. Nineteen-year-old Sandra Dubravcic, a Yugoslavian figure skater, lit the Olympic flame.

Lamija, eighteen, comes from Mostar, Bosnia-Herzegovina's second-largest city. Lamija's father is a major political figure in the country where he represents the Muslim party.

Lamija describes what it's like being the daughter of a politician in a country at war and how her family's safety is constantly in jeopardy. When a person comes to the United States as a refugee, he or she often seeks political asylum. Asylum means a place where one is safe. And, in Lamija's case, her need for safety is strongly felt.

5
LAMIJA
THREATS ON MY FATHER'S LIFE

My name is Lamija. I am from Mostar. I came to Boise, Idaho, five months ago as an exchange student. My family is still in Bosnia and Croatia. My mother lives with a friend in Croatia, and my older brother goes to college there. My father goes back and forth a lot between the two countries.

I lived in Croatia as a refugee for a year before I came here. I was living with a family friend, so I really didn't feel like a refugee. I left Mostar because my parents were afraid for me. I didn't want to go. I was 16 at the time. My mom said to me, "I don't want you to feel all of this and remember it all your life, so go ahead and go." I only experienced the actual war in Bosnia for about two months.

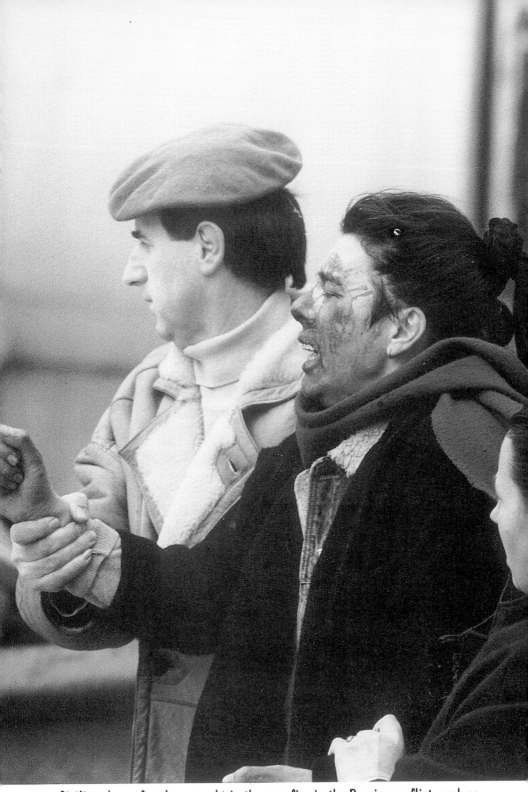

Civilians have often been caught in the crossfire in the Bosnian conflict, such as this Sarajevan woman who was hurt when shells were dropped on a crowded market.

I talk to my mom on the phone, because there is peace in Croatia and I can get through. She lives in a small town called Vrgorac. It's close to Mostar, even though it's in another country. When I was living there, my father traveled a lot between Bosnia and Vrgorac.

He is a politician. He's a pretty important figure in Bosnia right now. That's another reason my parents sent me out of town. Being a politician is dangerous.

My father was president of the Muslim Political Party for Herzegovina. He was quite close to the president of Bosnia, Alija Izetbegovic. Sometimes threats were made on my father's life. He is a really optimistic man and he believes in life, so he never talked about it much. Every time he went out he would have at least two people walking with him.

My mother is a professor of chemistry. She used to teach in the military school. The school was mostly Serb. When my father started in politics, they began hassling her at the school, so she had to leave. Then she started teaching at a high school in Mostar.

My father has been a politician ever since the Communist system began to break down. Before that, he used to have his own company. He always worked for himself, because he never trusted communism. He's really smart, and he's a good scientist. But because he didn't believe in the system, the country never really supported him.

He has strong hopes for Bosnia-Herzegovina. He is a very optimistic man. He never talks about bad things. When we were still living in Mostar and the bombing would last all day long, he would come home from work at eleven or twelve o'clock at night, and I would talk to him. I was so afraid of the war, but he would put hope back into my life. I don't understand how he can be like that with all the things he goes through.

I'm not sure what I'm going to do at this point. I have a wonderful opportunity to stay here. Because I am Bosnian, I can get full asylum in the United States. That would be really good for me, because I could go to college. But then I really miss my family and I want to see them. I can go to college in Croatia if I want, because they have peace there.

It's a dilemma for me. If I stay here, I have some good chances. I'm a really good student; I could make something of my life, achieve something. But if I go back I would be with my family. They won't come here, because my father is committed to Bosnia and my mother doesn't want to leave. It will be a hard choice for me when I do decide where to go. I don't think my family will ever go back to Mostar. Our town is totally destroyed, leveled. There is nothing there.

I like the United States pretty much. It was kind of hard at the beginning, all the new people and everything. But now I have some pretty good friends, and that makes me feel better.

Canadian soldiers serve lunch to children in the Serb-controlled village of Ilijas.

Sometimes people here can be annoying because they don't even know where Bosnia is. Or they ask me stupid questions like, "Do you have candy in Bosnia? Do you have houses?" Most American teenagers don't understand that we had absolutely the same life they do.

I like my school and I am doing well. Not long ago there was a speech contest at Boise State University, and I represented my school. I won third place, and I'm a foreigner!

Sometimes it's hard being here alone. I live with a host family, and I get along with them pretty well, but it's not like being at home. I'll stay in Boise until the end of the school year and then I'll decide what to do next. I would like to go to college and study design or architecture.◆

Emza, a Muslim, is a talented young musician who has played the piano since the fourth grade. When Emza had to leave her city, Mostar, a lot changed for her. She suddenly found herself in Jacksonville, Florida. She goes to school there, but she struggles with learning English and she doesn't have access to a piano.

Emza is having a difficult time. Not only is the United States new to her, but imagine not being able to communicate or pursue interests, like music, that help in making friends.

Emza talks about the "old bridge," as they call it in Mostar. It is a beautiful footbridge, built in the Ottoman style, that spans the Neretva River in Mostar. It has been very important culturally, historically, and, during the Bosnian war, strategically. In November, 1993, the "old bridge" was shelled and destroyed by Croat forces.

EMZA
ESCAPING THE SNIPERS

My name is Emza. I am 14 years old. I am from Mostar, a very old city on the Neretva River. Mostar is the capital of Herzegovina. I came to Jacksonville, Florida, just four months ago with my mother, Emina, and my brother, Esmir.

We used to live right in the center of Mostar. It is a beautiful town with many bridges. The oldest bridge was built in 1566, when the Turks ruled the region. It is made entirely of stone. It was the only bridge standing when I left Mostar.

My first memory of the war, when I realized the war was beginning, was a big explosion near the Bosnian Army's military headquarters. A bomb was set off in a big van.

Another memory I have is the time my mother, my brother, and I had to spend three days in the basement of our building because snipers were shooting into people's apartments. While we were there some Croat soldiers came in and questioned everyone. They pointed a gun at my brother's head. I was crying. I was very scared. Luckily, nothing happened.

The different armies are fighting over the east side and the west side of Mostar. The Neretva divides the city. My grandmother and grandfather are still in Mostar. My grandfather is 86, and my grandmother is 72. We don't know how they are doing now. It's hard to get through by letter or by phone.

My family and I do not feel differently about nationalities because of the war, as some Bosnians do. My mother's good friend was Serbian. When the east side of the city was liberated from the Serbs early in the war, many of the Serbs were forced out of Mostar or put in jail. My mother's friend was put in jail.

Later in the war in Mostar, the Croats tried to force the Muslims out of the city, because they think that Mostar should be the capital of the Croat republic. This struggle is what forced my family and me from our home. My family is Muslim, but all the nationalities have suffered in this war.

I don't want to go back to Bosnia, but my mother does. She doesn't like the United States. She says the people here aren't friendly. My aunt, who is also a refugee, lives in Salt Lake City. She and my mother talk on the phone a lot. My aunt tells my mother that the people in Utah are very nice. They were invited over to the house of my uncle's boss; they have friends. Their son is in the eighth grade there, and his class made him a cake for his birthday. And their older son already has a job as a paper boy. They've been in Salt Lake City as long as we've been in Jacksonville.

In school, I have problems with English. I can't understand everything people are saying. So, I got an F in American government. It's not an interesting subject to me.

In Mostar, I went to a special high school for musicians. I played the piano and sang in the school choir. I started playing the piano when I was in the fourth grade. I haven't had the opportunity to play since I came to the United States. I hope I will be able to soon.

I don't want to go back to Mostar when the war is over. If I went back, I don't think I would see any of my friends. They're all gone. Everyone is leaving the city. It's too dangerous to live there.◆

Esmir is Emza's older brother. Esmir has a keen sense of events and their significance in the war. He is very methodical in his thinking and views his country from a complex historical perspective.

Esmir is intelligent and strong-willed. Beneath his cool exterior lies great anguish and rage about his father, who was badly wounded in the war. Self-confidence is a matter of survival for Esmir right now. It holds him together; it holds his family together.

ESMIR
A GUN AT MY HEAD

My name is Esmir. I live in Jacksonville, Florida. I came here from Mostar two months ago with my mother and my sister, Emza.

The big explosion in Mostar that my sister talks about was on April 6, 1992. All the buildings within 50 meters were damaged or destroyed. The Croats were responsible for the explosion. At that time, the military in Mostar was controlled by the Serbs; many of the soldiers were Serbs.

The first shooting in Mostar happened around April 10. It was nothing compared to those that came later. At first, I was so afraid that I couldn't sleep at night. Later, people got used to it; there was shooting all night and no one cared.

Mostar is in Herzegovina, in a valley of the Neretva River. It is completely surrounded by mountains and hills. Like all cities in Bosnia, Mostar was very cosmopolitan. Muslims, Serbs, and Croats all lived

together. There was also a small group of Jews.
Before the war, Mostar's population was 150,000.
It was the second-largest city in Bosnia-Herzegovina,
after Sarajevo. Now only 40,000 people live there.

When the war started, the Croats controlled the
area on the right, or eastern, bank of the Neretva,
which was mostly Muslim. The Serbs occupied all
the hills around the east side of the city. The Muslims on the western bank had very few arms, and it
took the Serbs only fifteen days to conquer that
part of the city. The west bank fell on June 15, 1992.

Our house was on the west side. On July 20,
1992, the Muslims and Croats led a big offensive
and managed to liberate a tiny strip of land along
the western bank. That was how we lived for one
year.

On May 9, 1993, the second war, between the
Muslims and the Croats, broke out and we were
no longer allies. The eastern bank and parts of
the western bank just along the Neretva were held
by Muslims, but there were also 20,000 Muslims
living in Croat-held parts. My house was right on
the front line between these territories. I could
look out on the front line from our living room.
Eventually, the building I lived in was destroyed.

When the second war started, my father was
wounded by an antiaircraft grenade that was fired
into our apartment building. The big bullet went
through the wall down to the floor, bounced back
up through the door and into the hallway through
a wooden chair my father was sitting on. It swept

Mostar residents cross the new iron bridge donated to the city by the British government. The bridge joins the east and west parts of the city.

through the bottom part of both his thighs, and the chair shattered. All the little splinters of wood went into his legs. He got blood poisoning.

It was hard to get him to the hospital, because all the hospitals were on the Croat-held side. Six days later, he was transported to a provisional hospital on the western bank, but they had no medication. When the Bosnian Army arrived, he was taken to a hospital on the eastern bank. He didn't get the surgery he needed until 15 days after being wounded. After spending two months in Mostar, my father was transported to a hospital in Zagreb, Croatia. Life for Muslims on the western bank was very difficult. There were about 20,000 of us on the west side of the river, and about 50,000 were in camps.

Refugees on a makeshift raft transport a car across the Neretva River.

One day the Croats tried to seize our building. There had been shooting all day, and we had to go down to the shelter in the basement because all the windows faced the Croat side. You couldn't move your head for fear of being shot by snipers.

I am 17, but I look older. My mother was often afraid for me. The Croat soldiers came into the shelter with guns. When a soldier asked me my name, I said, "Esmir Celebic." Then he asked, "Are you Muslim?" "Yes," I answered. All the while, he was pointing a gun right at my head. My mother was clutching my arm. Then he asked me if I was in the Bosnian Army, and my mother said, "Oh no! He's only sixteen years old!" My sister and I always tease her about how dramatic she is.

One day a boy from the Bosnian Army sneaked

into the building and found us. He asked if we

wanted to go to another part of town that was held by Muslims, a neighborhood called Cernica. This was all happening while my father was in the hospital; we had no idea how he was doing. To get across to Cernica, we had to cross a bridge.

Mostar had five bridges. During the first part of the war, the Serbs mined all the bridges in Mostar except the old stone bridge, built in 1566.

One day the old bridge was opened up to those who wanted to go to the east. That's when my mother, my sister, and I left. A few days later, it was closed again and we couldn't go back. We stayed with my aunt, my father's sister, on the east side.

The streets were filled with soldiers. Every night they would look into the houses and search all the apartments. They were looking for arms and for men. Any men over eighteen years were taken to the camps. We knew we had to leave.

The day I left Mostar, I went to my grandparents' house in a neighborhood called Brankovac to say goodbye. Brankovac was a famous Serbian poet from Mostar. He wrote during this century and was famous because he wanted Serbs and Muslims to be friends. The Turks had ruled Bosnia for 500 years. In the current war, the Serbs want to kill anyone who is a Muslim. It is their revenge.

UN officials transported us out of Mostar. We went to Croatia. In Split, we applied to the International Rescue Committee for help, and now here I am in Jacksonville. My father is still in Zagreb. He's out of the hospital now and coming here soon.

My father is a professor of history. He taught at the University of Mostar. His field involved cultural societies of Mostar from 1900 to 1950. He was also the curator of the archives of Herzegovina. My mother used to do electrical drawings for buildings. She worked at that job for 22 years and then was fired because she was Muslim.

Before the war, I never felt any tensions between people. We had friends who were Croats and Serbs. People didn't care what you were. After World War II, when Yugoslavia was created, the only way to keep the peace was to forget about nationalities.

I'm a senior in high school here. I'm the best in my class in Latin. Americans can't say some words in Latin, so when I say them all my classmates are amazed. I got an A in calculus two weeks after we got here. At that time I was six weeks behind, so I think that's pretty good.

I like my school here in the United States. I have made some new friends. I don't want to go back to Bosnia. I no longer have a home there. I don't have anything there. My whole family is here except for an aunt who is still in Sarajevo. None of my friends are there. Many of them will never go back. Mostar is dead now.◆

A man cycles by the evidence of heavy fighting in central Sarajevo. Often, sniper fire prevents parts of the city from being cleaned up.

Naida comes from Sarajevo, Bosnia-Herzegovina's major city. Before the war, life in Sarajevo was like that of many urban centers. People enjoyed the libraries, the museums, the cinemas, and the theater.

Sarajevo is the cultural dividing line between major religious and ethnic worlds. Before the war, many Sarajevans demonstrated a remarkable desire for integration. Many Sarajevans were proud of this accomplishment, and, like Naida, wanted it to grow. But the war in Bosnia has swept away the dynamic aspects of integration.

Naida spends a great deal of time thinking about the plight of her country. She has written about the war for *Newsweek* and has appeared on panels and at conferences around the country. She bears the intense pain of her shattered city and country with amazing strength and keen political insight.

NAIDA
A WAR FOR POWER

My name is Naida. I was born and raised in Sarajevo. I came to the United States in 1991 as a foreign exchange student. That was before the war broke out in Yugoslavia.

I am here by myself. My family is still in Sarajevo, my older brother and my mother. My father died four years ago. About every two months I get a letter from home. I don't know if they're getting enough food. I can only hope.

They won't come to the U.S. My mother is 55, and I don't think she would be willing to move. She is a doctor and works in a hospital in Sarajevo.

I just finished my freshman year at Western Maryland College in Westminster. I'm studying math on a four-year scholarship. It pays for my tuition, but I have to make money for room and board.

I work a lot right now, during summer vacation, in Essex, a suburb of Baltimore, where I live with a host family. I work 65 to 70 hours a week to save money to support myself next year at school. I'm a technical assistant at Johns Hopkins University. I help graduate students in the mechanical engineering lab. At night and on weekends I work as a hostess in a restaurant in Essex. It's a chain restaurant, not great, but okay. I get tired a lot.

I don't like living in the suburbs. It's really flat, boring, gray. I hate it that I need a car just to buy food. It's a ten-minute drive to the grocery store.

I like the area around my college better. There's a lot of greenery and hills. It looks like home. It's strange how much that means.

I saw the separation among the people of Bosnia starting about a year before the war broke out. Some people say they were preparing for war even ten years ago. I never thought Yugoslavians were preparing for war.

The rise in nationalism was a surprise to me. It was never present in me, or in my friends, and it never will be. I guess it was my generation that was most surprised by the war.

The problem in Yugoslavia is not that it is a religious war, as many people would like to think. It's a war for power. Certain factions have complete control of the press and the media. What you see on television in Serbia is totally different from what you see in Bosnia-Herzegovina or Croatia. They make the people in the villages believe it's a

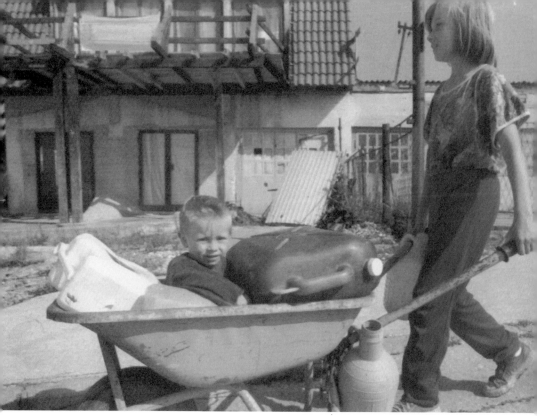

A Bosnian girl and her brother fetch water for their family in Sarajevo. The city has been under siege for almost three years and was without water much of the time.

religious war. If this were a war about nationality and religion, Croatia and Serbia wouldn't be making deals.

Bosnia was an integrated land. Forty percent of the people in Sarajevo have mixed marriages. It's less mixed in the country, but I never saw deep hatred between people there. The power lies with a handful of people. A lot of what they say is propaganda.

As far as nationality is concerned, I don't regard myself as anything, nor do I have any religious beliefs. I like to think of myself as an internationalist.

In Yugoslavia, people had a more relaxed way of being religious. My parents are both Muslims,

A French UN soldier helps a woman crossing a bridge in Sarajevo. United Nations troops have attempted to keep peace and monitor the Bosnian situation.

but not really religious. I guess they believed, but in a relaxed way.

In the fall I will go back to school in Westminster. I have to say, I think American college students are less serious than Bosnians. They only know about life in the U.S., nothing outside it. Maybe it's because they have parents and a home here. Because I'm a foreigner and alone, I have to take care of myself.

I am very angry at the international community's response to the war in Bosnia. They have been very passive, so unbelievably careless. It has been clear for two years how much aggression is going on and who is doing it, and they do nothing. I feel the world is responsible.

So far, I've been disappointed about actions taken here to stop the war. At a rally I went to in Washington, D.C., the people who attended were religiously oriented. There were Muslims, Christians, Jews. That's not the way to solve the situation. You don't solve this problem with religion or ethnicity, but by being human. Sometimes people seem to think I'm crazy, but I have many friends, all of different ethnicity and religion, who feel as I do. That is what gives me hope.◆

Glossary

atrocity Act of extreme wickedness or brutal cruelty.

Balkans The countries of the Balkan region: Romania, Bulgaria, Albania, Greece, European Turkey, and the former Yugoslavia; a center of political unrest for centuries.

ethnic Relating to large groups of people having common racial, cultural, tribal, or linguistic characteristics

ethnic cleansing Policy of ridding a region or country of members of all cultural groups but one, usually by military force.

indigenous Originating in a particular region or country; native.

Islam The religion of the Muslims, whose God is Allah and whose holy book is the Koran.

nationalism Assertion of the interests of a particular nation over those of other nations; excessive patriotism.

propaganda Information or rumors deliberately spread to promote a cause or to injure another cause.

refugee Person who flees his or her country because of war or persecution.

sanction A threat or fine designed to enforce a law or standard.

stoicism A lack of emotion or feeling.

tolerance A fair, accepting attitude toward persons of a race, nationality, or religion other than one's own.

For Further Reading

Andric, Ivo. *The Bridge on the Drina*. Chicago: University of Chicago Press, 1977.

Colakovic, Branko. *Yugoslav Migrations to America*. San Francisco: R and E Research Associates, 1973.

Dizdarevic, Zlato. *Sarajevo: A War Journal*. New York: Fromm, 1992.

Djilas, Aleska. *Contested Country*. Cambridge: Harvard University Press, 1991.

Dragnich, Alex. *Serbs and Croats: The Struggle in Yugoslavia*. New York: Harcourt, Brace, Jovanovich, 1992.

Drakulic, Slavenka. *Balkan Express: Fragments from the Other Side of War*. New York: Norton, 1992.

Filipovic, Zlata. *Zlata's Diary*. New York: Viking, 1994.

Glenny, Misha. *The Fall of Yugoslavia*. New York: Penguin, 1992.

Kaplan, Robert. *Balkan Ghosts: A Journey Through History*. New York: St. Martin's Press, 1993.

Thompson, Mark. *Paper House: The Ending of Yugoslavia*. New York: Pantheon, 1992.

Index

About the Author

Valerie Tekavec, author of a forthcoming book of short stories, *Peacocks and Beans,* is a freelance writer and translator. She is currently working toward her doctorate in German literature at the City University of New York Graduate Center. She teaches German poetry at Bard and German language at the State University of New York at New Paltz.

Ms. Tekavec lives in Woodstock, New York.

Photo Credits

pp. 12 and 30 © Valerie Tekavec; all other photos © AP/Wide World Photos

Layout and Design

Kim Sonsky